A LAST LOVING
Collected Poems

Maeve Kelly

A Last Loving
Collected Poems

ARLEN
HOUSE

A Last Loving:
Collected Poems

is published in 2016 by
ARLEN HOUSE
42 Grange Abbey Road
Baldoyle
Dublin 13
Ireland
Phone/Fax: 353 86 8207617
Email: arlenhouse@gmail.com
arlenhouse.blogspot.com

Distributed internationally by
SYRACUSE UNIVERSITY PRESS
621 Skytop Road, Suite 110
Syracuse, NY 13244–5290
Phone: 315–443–5534/Fax: 315–443–5545
Email: supress@syr.edu

978–1–85132–148–3, paperback

Typesetting by Arlen House

Editing by Alan Hayes

Cover artwork by Oona O'Brien Kelly
courtesy of Maeve Kelly

CONTENTS

9   *Acknowledgements*

11   *Introduction*
     Vivienne McKechnie and Jo Slade

NEW AND UNCOLLECTED
17   The Poet's Mother
19   Table Cloth
20   Oona
21   Memorial
22   Scribe
24   Friendship
25   Love
26   Voice
27   A Book
28   Ghost
29   Ancestry
31   A Lantern in the Dark
32   Fish
33   Our Country Mothers
35   Winter
36   Pacifist
37   The Question
38   Primo Levi's Prayer
39   Refuge
40   Mary
41   Give Me Tools
42   Snow in Winter
43   Dish
44   If I Were a Man
45   Amnesiac
46   Margaret

47   I Weep for This

48   Jessie's Song

49   Poem 28

50   After Rain

51   In Memoriam

52   Old Age

LAMENT FOR OONA (2005)

57   Angel

58   Death

59   First Day

60   Hearse

61   Lament

63   Song

64   Where Dark is Deepest

65   Once

66   The Woman who Laments

67   Christmas

68   If

69   Bird

70   Your Cat

71   What City Knows You Now?

72   Nothing

73   A Moment

74   Brother Job

75   The Fates

76   Time

77   Tomb

78   Healing

79   Love

80   Eagle

81   On Viewing a Painting, *Atrabilarius*, by Salcedo

83   Bonfire

84   Mirror

85   For a Coming Grandchild

86   Decade

87 Supermarkets
88 Journey
89 I Greet the Stars Early
90 Communion

RESOLUTION (1986)
95 Resolution
96 Love I
97 Mother Love
98 First Child
99 Creator
100 Clonmoney
101 Ballad of a Town
103 Daughter
104 Love II
105 Rescue
106 Words
107 Spring in Meelick
108 Geranium
109 Heretic
110 Wedding Picture
111 That Old Love Again
112 If I Forget
113 Inheritance 1970
114 Ireland 1972
115 Kin
116 Fear
117 For a Deaf Friend
118 Lament to Van Gogh
119 Book of Kells
120 Elegy for Mary Catherine
121 Today There was Rain Again
122 Feminist I
123 Spinster
124 Middle Age
125 Rationale

126 Functions
127 Noon-Day Tiger
129 Feminist II
130 New House
131 Half Century
134 Starlings
135 Horizons
136 Winter Day
137 Love Letter
138 Trees
139 For Sheila Gleeson
142 Cognomens
143 Winter 1983
144 Feminist III

146 *About the Author*

ACKNOWLEDGEMENTS

Thanks to Vivienne McKechnie and Jo Slade for their tireless work in ensuring this book would be published.

Much thanks to Maeve Kelly for agreeing to publish this book and for working with Vivienne and Jo in gathering material and finalising the introduction and biographical note. Thanks also to Maeve's brother Brian and her son Joe.

The publisher would like to thank Kevin Honan and Clairr O'Connor of Astrolabe Press who edited and published *Lament for Oona* for permission to reproduce these poems here.

INTRODUCTION

Vivienne McKechnie and Jo Slade

Lovers of and practitioners of poetry and literature in Ireland would agree that in the 1970s and 1980s Irish poetry underwent significant changes. These changes were propelled by a more general articulation of dissatisfaction and questioning within Irish society, especially by Irish women. Poets, writers and artists pick up on these anxieties; the best of their creative work responds to and transforms this disquiet and by so doing, makes it possible for us to see ourselves more clearly, to understand the complexities and subtleties of the human condition and to identify vulnerabilities and injustices.

Maeve Kelly's literary output is an important and impressive contribution to modern Irish literature, to that era, when women in particular, were giving new voice to the struggle for equality and recognition.

Beginning in the 1970s and up to today Maeve Kelly has published two volumes of poetry, *Resolution* (Blackstaff Press, 1986) and *Lament for Oona* (Astrolabe Press, 2005), two collections of short stories, *A Life of Her Own* (Poolbeg Press, 1976) and *Orange Horses* (Michael Joseph, 1990), two novels, *Necessary Treasons* (Michael Joseph, 1985) and *Florrie's Girls* (Michael Joseph, 1989) and a feminist novella, *Alice in Thunderland* (Attic Press, 1993) all of which have received praise and awards in Ireland and abroad. It is, however, through her poetry that we can identify the 'original' poetic voice that informs all of her work. Maeve's writing is much admired for its lyrical resonance but also because it is a reflection of her commitment to writing in pursuit of social justice and women's liberty. Her poetry affirms her lifelong endeavour to preserve the dignity of personal experience, to react and respond to injustice and also life's vicissitudes.

Writing in Ireland in the 1970s and 1980s and within a post-colonial culture where identification of power became synonymous with conservative ideologies, Maeve's poetry reclaims the importance of the individual. Her poetry represents an acknowledgement of the necessity for the authentic individual voice, a voice urgent to be heard and with affecting things to say.

It is true that her poetry is central to her life, it is the emotional 'soul' of all her writing and thinking. As she says, 'poetry springs out of some deep part of oneself and all poetry comes out of love'.

Maeve Kelly was born in Ennis, Co. Clare and educated in Dundalk. She trained as a nurse in St Andrew's Hospital, London and, after qualifying, worked in Oxford before returning to Ireland. For many years she lived and farmed with her husband Gerard O'Brien Kelly and children, Joseph and Oona, in Co. Clare. She later moved with her family to her home in Limerick where she has lived since 1973. These geographical shifts reflect a dis-ease, a restlessness that echoes in her work. Less obvious perhaps than her identity and concern with women's freedoms, but there nonetheless, this dis-ease, coupled with confinements as a child and young adult through illness, has made her a deeply reflective, serious writer.

As a poet Maeve Kelly has always had a strong connection to the natural world, its power and beauty, its dissolution. Maeve's greatest contribution to Irish literature however, in both her poetry and prose, is her ability to give voice to the ordinary, everyday lives of Irish women. She writes out of her own experience as a woman, wife, mother, nurse, farmer and feminist activist and has always been an astute witness to the narrow confines of home and the limitations imposed by Irish society on women. Her language, her expression moves beyond those confines, looks outward with urgency, searching for resolution.

Feminist principles inform her poetry and her prose and these concerns continue to be explored and developed throughout her career. As an ardent campaigner for women's rights and through her writing Maeve Kelly is an important voice in the discourse of Irish women's activism. Her commitment has always been resolute and is evident by her involvement as a founding member and administrator for fifteen years of Adapt House in Limerick, a shelter for women who are victims of violence in the home.

If, as Maeve Kelly says, 'all poetry comes out of love' then surely her second collection of poetry, *Lament for Oona* (Astrolabe Press, 2005) is testament to one of the greatest loves, that of a mother for her child. This beautifully produced book, with reproductions of Oona's paintings and drawings, is a passionate lament, an outpouring of grief at the death of a daughter. These poems delve into the darkest reaches of the psyche to try to retrieve the lost or at least to remember the beloved, and by so doing give a kind of form to grief, and therefore hope.

In the previously uncollected poignant poems here, Maeve contemplates old age with compassion and courage. To those who already know and love Maeve Kelly's short stories, novels and poetry, this publication, her collected poems, brings together poetry that spans a lifetime. Through fifty and more years, Maeve has chronicled her journey; she has confronted its challenges and been an exceptional advocate of women's rights. These poems testify to that.

Limerick,
December 2015

... Her feet dancing to birdsong ...

A LAST LOVING:
COLLECTED POEMS

THE POET'S MOTHER

The poet spoke gently of his mother,
tenderly he remembered her hands
sudsy deep amid her prosaic pots,
graciously he recalled her kitchen
misty with broth, frescoed with peelings
and over all an unnoticed music –
the intimate scrape and burr of cleaning.

Between them grew, rank and deep, the rift
of their experience. Their sex faltered
at the brink of a division
as wide and high as canyon.
Although they touched over lettuce leaves
and communed in silence
by the carved Sunday joint
each recoiled from a disturbing chasm.
The generations surged between.

I would like to hear from the poet's lips
what was the tune his mother hummed
as she carried pails of milk from the byre
or stopped at a gateway and lightly turned
to look at a sky. I wish he would recall
all she said to her neighbours after Mass
and what she said of her birthing pangs
when he had ruptured their secret seal
and launched, a ship bursting free
from safe moorings to reckless seas.

Did she say: After him I bled for days.
I wished to die and almost one night
felt myself slipping away. His cry

brought me back. I felt his need
and I returned from a peaceful place
of deep valleys and wooden hills and falls
of water chiming like crystal bells.
Here I have been since, between kitchen and yard
pondering many things in my heart.

I should like to hear all that from the poet.
I would like to see a lost girl's look
caught in the clever pen of her son.
I would like to feel that he understood
that strange grammar of her heart,
her bright mind's declension.

TABLE CLOTH

The stitches of her tablecloth
have web-like caught
the ninety years since she was born.

Serene as silver on old lace
awaiting mealtime talk
her picture smiles above the knives and forks.

New generations she has never seen
argue old battles she has never fought,
debate with wine the politics of fear,
digest with camembert the alien north.

Her subtle artistry is here ignored.
The tracery of her life's design
crumples and fades like women's words
among the rougher arguments of men.

The blood of grapes has spread its stain
upon her thought. Her words, unsaid,
are written epics where young elbows lean
destined as usual to be unread.

After the meal I wash and starch
her love's memorial. I fold and put away
the linen shroud that is her art.
I store in cupboards all she had to say.

OONA

She was all those colours
we bear in memories.
Autumn in the chestnut of her hair,
her skin, like the moon waning
luminous on water,
her eyes lit with the glow of summers.

Her feet dancing to birdsong.

Winter came at the end.
All her life's mystery sealed
under its veil.
We stepped back in dark
and abandoned our cries.

MEMORIAL

It is not that I regret my anger.
The gush of tears, the noise
of grief, its high pitch
banishing words.

I soothe my brain
with images of hyacinths
in a dark cupboard,
their scent when ripe
too strong for death,
their candle blossoms
voluptuous with life.

Now I learn silence.

SCRIBE

Unwashed at a breakfast table,
as a man might be unshaven,
though with no overgrowth of stubble,
I take my pen in hand,
with the same accident in mind.

From the heart and head's confusion
to create a union of both,
my hard thought's sandpaper
abrasive on the soft growth
sprouting from too much feeling.

Too much felt. Too much thought.
That was a waltz I danced
with two left feet, too much intent
of purity at the core
so that all
peripherals must be ignored.

Crooked or wrong,
an unmetred song,
my poem says nothing
of seeds sown
of women in love
of men's hard taking.

Of old murders with new names,
of shattered skulls,
or lacerated skin,
the litter of war games,
of why a severed head
or a toe-nail cut
should merit the same regret.

What is the other in me? My poem
marks its un-rhythm to that tune,
the out-of-step, undiscovered,
the blind, unreached-for plan,
mocking in tandem its unseen twin
love-death. Life-decay.

This is the furnace around which I dance,
its heat teaching me the balance
even the planets must practice.

I am a scorched shadow in its flame,
a frozen spectre in its shade.

FRIENDSHIP
for Jo

A poem well made
sits in the soul like a bird

whose nest lies over the trouble of cats,
who peers out with question marks
written over its gaze.

Do you love me, it asks,
am I safe to come out?
Friendship is sacred,
I hold it in my hand.
A sacred host,
I take it in.
I tap its spring.

This is our gift to one another.

We break bread together.

LOVE

I embraced these chains.
Their spikes tore me.

You need food,
therefore I cook.

I need order,
therefore I clean.

My poems lie unborn
on my unmade bed.

VOICE

The souls of the dead venture far
bringing our prayers with them.
Our candles are lit,
our flowers are placed.
Our dreams invade your dreams
and when we sleep
your voice sings again.

A BOOK

My memory is my sustenance.
It feeds my spirit's growth,
it labours to support the flower
my grief for you brought forth.

I am its source, its stem and root.
Without me it must fade.
Therefore I plant it in a book
where death may turn its page.

GHOST

Communing with the ghost of your past,
the guessed presence you became,
unfathomable yet truly known,
even to the marrow of my bone.
I cannot bid you farewell.

ANCESTRY

Though stars dissolve in time
to empty their impenetrable hearts
in the core of themselves,

we may journey past,
singing of the times we knew
when earth was green and whole.

We will remember then
the sweetest dawns of spring,
our suns dispersing mists

on shiny pearls of water,
ancient crafts of ironwork and wood,
weaving, hammering, cutting,

scripts engraved in stone
or printed on papyrus.

We will remember
the naming of seasons,
the passing of a life.

One little day an infant knows
before she yields her breath
one little moment

when her mother's eyes
meet its questioning gaze,
even that

will be remembered by our dust.

In the great stillness after all is done,
the empty universe will hold
an echo of what life has been.

When all the stars put out their lights
and all our skies are black,

one spark
may kindle forgotten thought
and blaze into existence once again.

We are spectators at the gates.
Even as the day ends
we attend the future.

A LANTERN IN THE DARK
for Gerard

I have shut the shutters,
clipped the locks
and put the cat out,
kissed your beard
and helped you to your bed.
Eighty now and the years
bend you like a bow,
a sprung arch,
a willow wand,
bones chiselled to a new arc.

Sweetheart I know
the way you grow
not old but with your old
lightness still showing,
a lantern swinging in the dark.

FISH

An opalescent, translucent shape,
the jellyfish floats under a sky of water.
On the pier wall I observe with wonder
his sensuous marriage to sea,
being of it, yet moving free
as the limpid blue hills are free
of air and blue sky and white
cloud. And this pale pearl,
this purest mushroom of sea flesh
born where seaweed waves like coral,
deep below the stone steps,
moves indolently towards the rope
tethering curragh to bollard.
It floats upside down,
liquefied parachute, pluming
slow as a lover easing after
love making on a cushioned bed,
unfolds white trails, slender
pale lines. Fonds and flowers
are cousins to this fish,
petals of silk unfolding to a kiss
of honey bee, or ancestor a cloud
simmering in a sea where stars keep
patient vigil over death.

Worked to the bone they said they were,
our country mothers and their mothers too.
Signs on it, when they rested in old age,
they were not apple cheeked and plump, but true
to breeding showed their bones skin taut
on Roman noses and on parchment hands
eyes bright with scorn, remembering how they fought
the bitter weather and the stony lands,
while softer daughters home from Yankee States
trailed loving husbands, grumbling all the while
about the rain, the wind, the smoky kitchen grates
and how they had to walk a half a mile.

My grandmother fetched water every day,
first from the well for drinking, this was sweet
flavoured with ferns and hazel boughs and fresh
from mountain heather where the rainstreams meet.
Next to the soft bog lake she'd bring her pails,
dipping between the water lilies and the lordly reed,
pausing a while to hear the drunken sound
of cuckoo hiccoughing in sheltered weeds.
Today there is a memory of that daily walk,
stretching from house to water lily bed,
a fuschia hedge she planted stalk by stalk,
signs of her labour in each purple head.

Yet often she would smile amid her toil,
and think of how her mother spent her days,
and how on market day a man from Boyle
once gave her what she said was purple praise
because her butter packed in firkin tight,
tested by skewer never failed to be
superb in texture and in flavour right,
and she was praised for this consistency.

I have a vision of her often in my mind,
my mother's mother long ago,
her kitchen chairs and tables scrubbed to white,
the lime washed walls kept shining as the snow.
And when I hear men sing the patriot dead,
I think of how their mothers spent their days,
and wish that once or twice some laurelled head
would rise and give her, due and public praise.

WINTER

Constant as the impermanence allows,
the fragile days of winter have appeared,
have shaken lusty greenery from the boughs,
with icy breath the later roses seared.
Pale fingers crystallise the window pane,
and brittle bright the night air glows,
pale skies with wispy colouring contain
the delicate reflection of far snows.
Scavenging winter has laid waste the woods,
stripping her glory from the noble beech,
baring to mockery the defiant oak,
snatching the acorn from the squirrel's reach.
All's silhouette and bare boned to the sky.
All's harsh and unrelenting to the view,
the landscape shivers naked to the eye.
Earth's poverty is pitifully true.

PACIFIST

I shut my mind to the thought of war.
Offensive the smell that is its very essence,
the smell of death triumphant.
Coward I am to so exclude the thought,
since war is merely Phoenix in its ashes,
and death blows the Victor's trumpet.
Well coward I am and choose to be.
I fear the dreadful subtleties of courage,
the arrogance that leads to selfish bravery.
What does it matter if a man may rise
bigger and stronger than his pre-slaughtered?
Better a dead planet mocking the skies
than the fertile plains be watered
by the rich minerals of spilled blood.

Man is improvident of his seed,
a wastrel constantly spending.
How could he know, who merely cast it into darkness
and never knew the harshness of the reaping
nor ever heard the voice of the reaper weeping.
War mocks a woman's pain, but asks acceptance,
war is a plausible beggar, a thief, a cheat.
Hold back your tears, from this there's no deliverance.
Rally brave comrades and smile when the beggar you meet.
Terence McSweeney said it, but he spoke to a world deranged.
'My enemy is my brother from whom I am estranged'.

THE QUESTION

Whether it was worth it
becomes the question,
harsh and graceless now
tattooing.
Persistence is a drill
to pierce me
through more than skin
into the inner heart.
It comes and goes
unanswered,
you might be pained to hear.

What does your photo say?
A gleaming glance at eight,
flower in the garden,
at twenty still amused.
Your look does not assuage,
does not bequeath,
crumb comforts, says only,
you were here, enough
that life lent lustre to your hair.

PRIMO LEVI'S PRAYER

If I was God
I would spit at Kuhn's prayer
who knelt on his bunk
his beret on his head
praising his God
because he had not been chosen.

When the copper rain came down
the blood on the paving stone
ran to meet it.
They flowed together
and rushed to the hungry one who waited.

The sea will open its mouth
to swallow their endeavour
and when the burnt cities have decayed
and all the rivers have dried,
only the fool will say,
we will remember them forever.

REFUGE

He touched me here – she said
laughing, the red hair swinging
to hide her pale surprise
and she laced her fingers
over the mound of her child
on each side again, the sphere
of her inner world concealed
and then revealed by her light
mannerly exposition.

In the centre aisle of the church
in front of all – she said – he placed
his hands here. I was mortified.
And that smile again, confused
yet awed by tribute, seemed to light
our table where we hung, silent
over empty tea cups. A child cried
in a room upstairs and one moved
to listen. Outside the orange glare
a security light zoned our limits,
a rubbish tip where horses roamed
wild as their owners, illicit nibblers
at our crooked pastures.
We here are tenants. There in the church
the priest proclaimed, not her
but her inhabitant, mysterious life.

She was bemused by this.
This spotlight on her portion,
her definable other
the source of her significance.
She hung her head, and we hung with her
speechless.

MARY

Creation moved the waters of my womb
and in that tumult voices cried aloud,
cried to be heard above the pain of life
ushering in the shadow of the shroud.
The wailing of the world beat at my door,
calling for justice, peace and food.
Yet I was born as ignorant and poor
and hungry as that hungry multitude.
I will not let them in though they weep a million years
for they will take the life that I have made,
will bleed it dry and grind it into dust
and make an image of the thing they slayed.
In some poor peasant's pocket,
two thousand years from now
the life that stirs within me will be shown,
not curled in tender care beneath my heart,
nor king-like seated on a kingly throne,
but stark on timber with his limbs transfixed,
a pitiless symbol for a pitiless world,
fingered by grimy thumb when Angelus tolls six.
'And the Word was made Flesh, and the Word
dwelt among us'. O Word, remain unsaid.
O Life, stay still unborn.
The hands outstretched for bread
will impale you on a thorn.

GIVE ME TOOLS

Give me tools, I asked the woods
and I will carve a poem.
I'll chip and dig and hew
and make a new branch grow.

We cannot help, the forest sighed.

Try stones or clay
for they will make an empty room
where you may sew
a garment that your words can wear
to Wedding Feast or Requiem Mass.
Be patient and your flesh will grow
as old as any limb of mine
and when it falls in its own time
we both will moulder and decay.

SNOW IN WINTER

I would like the snow to fall in winter,
goose down from a God's wife
plucking feathers in her basement kitchen.

It would be pure
not blood stained from a broken quill
nor tainted with the dirt of her floor.

That is our pollution.

Snow would muffle the sounds of war.
Leave US planes grounded at Shannon.
Stifle. Shock. Awe.

Snow would forgive all,
would hold us in its white hand
until repentance came.

Instead, winter slides into summer
without a by-your-leave.
Birds compete with calls for dominion,
trees wild with discovery,
daffodils aghast at their own beauty.

We are blasted by sunshine,
unseasonal, miraculous.
We are too old and wise
for such uneasy liberation.

DISH

I am my own dish.
Potted clay
shaped by pain.
I lap up grief,
dip into its pit,
write my script
on water and drink
myself in it.
I am grief's leper.
I smell of him.
His odours on my skin
place me in quarantine.

IF I WERE A MAN

If I were a man born of woman
I would sit outside the gates of my Jerusalem.
The stubble of my beard would prick my skin
and I would scrape my hair from off my head
with the shin bone of a slaughtered goat.
I would weep into the waters of the Nile
and on my loins I'd wrap a camel skin.
I'd raise my voice against the desert winds
and swallow all its vengeful dust.
But I would never be a poet,
to scrabble in the mire of words,
to take a thought and call it art
and preen myself upon my heap of dung
to glorify the deeds of men.

If I were a man born of woman
I would sit outside the gates of my Jerusalem.
I would shave my head and grow my beard
until it hid my manhood.

I would weep
until my tears washed the feet
of all the women who gave me birth.

Amnesiac

Amnesiac, I open to the conscious day
with harness strapped.
A new survival kit,
I try to encounter it.

My dreams carve chasms,
push to wakefulness,
until subsidence turns them,
makes them artifacts.

MARGARET

Margaret has undyed her hair,
or so she said. Bright as brass
the old head. This hue
matches her sombre stare.
It goes with her resolve,
dark as mutiny and as deep.
Never again, she says,
never again will I
sit with that sour man,
eat his stale bread,
be rubbed raw by pain,
share his hard bed,
suffer this bruised skin.
He'll brand me no more.
Therefore,
said Margaret,
I have undyed my hair
so that he'll know
I'm no longer his whore.

I WEEP FOR THIS

I weep for this
insensate brute in him.
In her the sharp cat
clawed somewhere in.
Insider, striving for out.

Outsider, guarding the gate,
he is planted, scowled,
sentinel, will not budge an inch.
She must climb on him
as cat climbs a tree,
may reach to his farthest limb,
then leap to be free.

Between them not a word.
He, schooled to indifference,
is numb to pain. He learned well
how to switch off nerve. Synapse
is the word. A leap to grief.
Minute span. Countless
bridges are crossed
by other torments. But not here.
Not with him.
Everything has shut down.
Everything has gone.

JESSIE'S SONG

Jessie shakes all over now
since they did that thing,
since they took electric wires
and plugged them to her brain.

Jessie's feet go suffering slow,
her memory's gone away.
She lies awake for half the night
and sleeps for half the day.

Jessie's husband beat her well
for that's what some men do.
He didn't like her woman's smell
or the way her baby grew.

He called her cunt and slut and whore
and cracked her off the wall
and when she cried he gave her more
then blamed her for it all.

Jessie's husband blamed his wife,
her children blamed their mother.
When she tried to take her life,
they didn't like the bother.

The doctor gave her Valium
and said she was depressed
and then he plugged her cranium
and – well, we know the rest.

Jessie shakes all over now
since they did that thing.
Since they took electric wires
and plugged them to her brain.

To be dumb with pen
is the stricken curse
of the grief worn,
is the fate of women
who enter childhood
with their father's demons
humping their backs.
They hear the music
that the word makes
deep within their souls
but when
they pick a thought
to run with it
they are
club footed
and stumble.

To be born blind to pen
is a slighter curse,
for mind
needs no eye to see
what it does not hear.
The heart must know its voice,
if it cannot praise, will curse,
and we who wander near
will catch the blight.

As the firethorn dies
when the wild spores descend
shriveling berry and bloom.

So will our bright poem.

After Rain

After a day of rain
light seems miraculous.
Everything shines twice,
pools black and sleek on roadsides.
A cluster of finches
shake feathers out to dry.
Footpaths gleam.
We submerge
in essence of pearl.
The river melts into the sky.

IN MEMORIAM
11 December 2013
Gerard

My love and my delight.
My heart's treasure.
My soul mate.
My comfort in distress.
My shelter from the storm.
My laughter maker.
My torch at midnight.
My sweet singer of songs without tunes.
Be with me always.

OLD AGE

When we become what we were;
silent, a curled embryo lost inside
the great womb of the world.
Before all this, before
the prattle of tongues,
before the eyes that stare
vacant over our heads,
we know
that it is time to go.

LAMENT FOR OONA

in memoriam
Oona O'Brien Kelly
1968–1991

One snowdrop under a cherry tree
does not celebrate a victory
for its unrivalled whiteness.
It is a promise
thrust from dark earth.

ANGEL

When you came through the door
wearing your purple hair
I thought you were an angel.

How could I know
that under your delicate bones
wings were growing?

How could I guess
the parabola of flight
that took your spirit?

Or dream the arc your body made
when you flew from me?

DEATH

Round every corner
he stood and watched
a layabout with one desire
to catch you as you passed.
By river banks
by deep rock pools
by high sea cliffs
while I held on to you
your little hand in mine
my arms around your waist
your head against my breast.

And you,
safe as the house we nested in
with its lime trees
and silver birches
and chestnuts grown from conkers.

Maybe, he thought,
she has left the sweet lawns they mowed
the hollyhocks
they grew for luck
the whitethorn they kept
to ward off the evil wish
the malevolent look
and the bad thought

and never cut it.

Maybe he waited
until my back was turned,
until I thought
my worrying was over.

FIRST DAY

That was the First Day.
The day we drove
tyres skimming along wet roads,
hearts pulsing to a new rhythm,
the silent beat of weeping.
That was the day we came
into the inner room
passing the place where he lay
sheeted on his bier
his eyes fatally closed
his dead flesh forecasting our doom.

That was the First Day
the last of March
a day raw with the chill of winter.
Daffodils in our garden
bent their fragile necks
before the hurrying blast.
A cold Easter. The choir sang
Alleluia. The white Eucharist
was raised in blessing.

Note: The body of the young driver
of the motorcycle lay in the front room
of the mortuary. We had never met him.

HEARSE

When you were lifted from the hearse
a swan rose from the river.
I felt its wing beat in my breast.
I knew the purpose of its flight.

It was like nothing known
before or since,
because no birth
could prepare us for this.

LAMENT

When the sun rose on Easter Day
we saw you, laid on marble.
Your soft hair hid the stain
where Death's hand struck you down.

Our ravaged gaze was only for you
for the bloom of winter on your brow
for the wild honey hidden in your eyes
for your lips' tender curve
for the fading glimmer of your hair
for the moonshine in your skin.

Now I look for you in lands without season
in pools full of empty shells
where the small red crab hides
and the lugworm wriggles in his cave.

If a bird ruffles its wings I cry.
There she is!
If a petal lifts to a passing dragonfly
I call. Look! Quick!
If a worm turns in its blind coil
I whisper. See her. Here she is.

I am caught in grief's net,
flung in air so dense with pain
my bright gills wheeze
and drown my breath.
I am played for death's fool.
He reels me in
and schools me to his whim.

But luminous as a fish
you float transcendent
in seas of pearls.
Comets are chariots
you ride smoothly,
a free skater on ice,
kind as silk
caressing your bones.

SONG

Time moves to circle round the space
your life and mine once occupied
as interwrought as bark and bole
as grass and clover, breath and kiss
as stalk and leaf
as cloth and thread
as sea spray and the tide.

I walk again your infant steps
and call your name in prayer.
I want to wrap you in my arms
and fold you to my breast.

WHERE DARK IS DEEPEST

I fell into a place of no breath
where the dark is deepest.
My spirit went in search of yours
where sunlight cannot enter
where the roots of trees
are the arches of the skies
where moles burrow in vain
where no prayers are heard
and the Gods are silent.

I cannot remember the winters
and the summers have passed like strangers.
You do not know how heavy the silence lies
or how it drifts like snow through every room,
sending a chill through my bones.

Above my head I hear only rain.

ONCE

I had a child once
whose face was sun to me
and I her pale moon
orbited round her.

I knew her hair
as the swan knows
the downy plume of her cygnet
and hides her safe
from the roar of water.

I had a child once
I knew her face
as the river bank
knows the primrose
nestling in its breast
above the roar of water.

A beast gnaws at my breast bone.
It knows where to sink teeth
to feed its appetite.
It has a lust for grief.

THE WOMAN WHO LAMENTS

Your child, they said
is a candle in our house.
So she blessed them with it.

Now they warm their hands
by their own fireside
and their pity is a cold blast
that chills her path.

Absence fills your room.
It colours walls with a wash of light,
touches the place where you slept.

I hear your step in the hall.
Your breath fogs the windows.

The oak you helped me plant
climbs to your window,
confident of growth.

Summer survives
only to hide its shame
as leaves and blooms arrive.

CHRISTMAS

All of this is superfluous;
the energy of feast days
crass talk of politics
busy deeds of money dealing
giving and taking.
In the wet meadow a cow's mournful head
droops like an abandoned ghost.
Hollies flaunt berries of blood
while in the tallest birch
a thrush dances for his mate.

Cars rumble on the highway to Clare.

Acres of leaves are turning into mulch.
Soon primulas will rise, golden and showy
as vigorous as Christ after long burial.
The naked trees
stretch their unburdened limbs
and pray for a new Messiah.

I dream of you
minute by minute.
My thoughts turn round you
in and out
unwinding your sweet life.
I make a shroud
to wrap you round
lay you in my heart
where you belong.

Footsteps and shadows haunt the garden paths.

If

I will bind my pain into a sheaf
I will winnow it and grind it
I will offer all to death
I will give my sorrow up.
I will abandon every grief.

I will leave my gift upon his step
I will put my head into his mouth
if he brings me to your place
if he lets me put my palms
on your face
if he shows me where you are
if he lets me wind your hair
in the fingers of one hand.

BIRD

Somewhere between sky and earth
a bird waits, its throat slit
for a penny song. Its wings
beat the air to make a sound
the wind may whistle to.
Iron woman and mute bird
frail feather and hard rod.
Both hold up the sky.

I wish
your little bones could lie
under my skin. I wish I could grow
my flesh over them. I wish my tears
could wash away the smell of death.

YOUR CAT

The day is re-born.
Outside a blaze of summer
melts to indifference.

Yesterday your cat
nested in a hedge
a small dead bird near him.

I wept all night.
You lie, little bird,
under death's paw.

Your cat
whose ancestor was model for a sphinx
remembers nothing.
Know-all, his pose is regal
as sand-sifted archipelago.

Between earth and sky
he contains the two
in his delinquent stare.

An expert in strategic plans
he lies in an economy of space
a folded curl of bliss.
His stillness is a trance
to hypnotise the yellow leaf
whose grasp upon its universal tree
is finally cut loose.

I wish I were your cat.

WHAT CITY KNOWS YOU NOW?

What city knows you now?
What bird turns its quick head
to the sound of your passing?
What street throws your shadow
into artful relief?
What wind strings a song
to your lost voice?

Once the cities had glass domes
and the bridges were lovely
over rivers brimful of fish.
We caught them with silver nets.
Our boats were furnished with gilt
topaz and pearl.
There were pools on country roads
and the hedgerows bloomed.
Shyly the star flowers gleamed.
Seas lapped golden on the blue globe.

Is fada an lá,
and the nights longer
and my wail heard only by the dog
who lifts his head and howls in sympathy.

NOTHING

What if we are nothing after all,
no more than a smudged thumb print
like the mark your father left on the wall
as he went by to wash at the sink?

With hand as bold as death's
and with as plain a mission
I cleaned the imprint off
and wiped away his passing.

So easy then for death to take his cloth
and wipe away your breath,
remove the shadow that your spirit left
in every room, in cat's green eye
even in the frocks
hung like waifs astray in your old press
and in your dolls
lolling in their box.

Words carve channels in my skull
searching for silence.
It holds your presence
as the moon held the step
that first disturbed its dust.

A MOMENT

Passing the hall
I saw the blue brilliance
of a flower in a bowl
and caught again in passing
acute memories of you
and was comforted by a rose
sumptuous in display
perfect in its presence, shape and scent
arrangements of petals,
exact fall of its leaf.

BROTHER JOB

Job made room for me.
He moved over on his ash heap
to share his space.
Rheumy eyed, leprous skinned,
flaking like dead moths
into a thousand wings,
we picked scabs together,
longed for death, moaned in unison,
claimed innocence of wrong-doing,
contended with the One,
complained of being curdled as cheese
and swallowed our sour spit
with the fervour of wine tasters.

Job and I, comfortless,
comforted each other.
Sweet brother
shared with me his affliction.
A gift beyond reckoning.

THE FATES

And even as the dreaded Fates
slunk towards our garden gate
I put my mind to recreate
a world all seasons could accommodate.

Facing north, one wilful day in March
I routed down a sapling oak
pulled from a rock beside Lough Derg
in Brian Boru's fort.
Twisted and spindly, it repaid my care
by stretching out its arms in such desire
the birds abandoned the embracing sky
and rested in its breast.

Its roots went deep
and in due time bore acorns which it dropped
like children clustering round its feet.
I thought the tree would watch
our children's children grow
up its branches to its heart.

Our ignorance was blessed.
We skipped past dragons sleeping in their lair.
We heard them snort
and glimpsed the smoky signals of their rage
but thought them distant and forgot to fear.

What prayer could help us rise to face this day
or put our minds to anything but despair?

TIME

One can hear a door close
without noticing the hand
on the clock has stopped,
that the sun has dropped
a curtain over the trees
and the birds have stopped singing.

Today I stitched in place
your rag doll's button eyes.
I washed her petticoats
and laid them out to dry.

Her limbs akimbo in the sun
were bleached snow white.
Serene, this dumb princess
smiled at the summer sky.

A million years hence
a child full of your grace
may light a blessed candle
or hold a lily against her heart
bending her slender neck to its embrace
sending such a shaft of wonder
through the heart of her mother
that the sunlight on her hair will fade
and the clouds over new planets
will hold back their thunder.

TOMB

This house hears no laughter
pealing from an upstairs room.
Silence reaches to the rafters.
Cold stretches from the tomb.

Grief is a ragged toy
I play with night and day.

HEALING

The cuckoo nests behind Capantymore.
He rings out his bold salute
without fear or favour.
Perhaps you hear him.
I no longer dread his cry
seeing him marked with death
feeling fragile shells crushed
as the nest is emptied.

The grass is scented.
Seed pods swell.
The oak tree we planted
nourishes acorns.
I stand under its shade
and admire abundance.
I see your profile
etched between earth and sky.

Some call this healing.
Where it came from I cannot tell,
as if a cloak were thrown
to hide the shadows,
allow sunlight to enter
and frost to melt
as if my heart softened in its heat
like liquid wax shaping candles
that rediscover light.

LOVE

For us you changed the colour of the sky
illumined with saffron and rose
the greyest day, and when
garden petals folded and closed
and the weeds on paths were hoed
and piled on heaps to be carried away
we lit ceremonial fires of praise,
locked doors and gates
and brought love inside.

EAGLE

When the great eagle entered our lair
his wingbeat hushed the night.
The dark was not as black as his heart
and the frost not as cold as his eye.

When he carried you with him
his spittle fell on our roof.
It rotted the timbers and blocked
the chimney and filled our mouths with ash.

I saw they were shoes
held tight in muslin bags.
Each embraced the other
like devoted lovers
not waving or shouting salutes
but silent and stern.
They had gathered in heaps
among branches and leaves
plastic cans, ragged strips of cloth.
And once among them floated a hand
with two fingers missing.
When they were harvested one by one
or still on the feet that wore them
they became the silent ones
whose throats cannot sing
whose feet do not dance to old tunes
who will not hurry to school or prayer
or to buy black beans in the village store.
When the flood came their mothers watched from the shore
smiling to see what the current bore:
toy boats bobbing on the tide
out for a Sunday sail?
They waved as their flesh floated by.

Now every day they thank God that they have come so far
though their journey was terrible and haunted by fear.
They could scarcely lift their heads to check the star that
    beckoned them.
They moved like burdened beasts
their backs bowed under the weight of their past.
They bent so low it seemed the earth must claim them.
They never rested. At night they heard each other groan
and could not offer comfort

but turned this way and that
to escape the sound of grief.
Once they saw a gleam of light.
It pierced the gloom and their hearts stopped their frantic
   beat
and they whispered, Look.
This moment we remember Peace.

BONFIRE

The shoes of the dead are empty.
Though they walk in daylight
they leave no print behind.
The shoes of the dead gather no dust.
They wait like dogs at the door.
Sometimes a man comes to check them.
Are you still here? he asks and weeps.
He picks them up one by one
and holds them to his face.
He smells the broken lace and the cobbled soles
and lays them out in rows.
He matches pairs and counts till all are gone.

The shoes of the dead march in silence
to the place where he cannot go.
He remembers their pace,
their dancing for joy.
He watches the smoke on their funeral pyre
filter through hedges and rise past trees.
I stand by the window and see the red glow
of the journeys you made
where your father stands bowed
as they flicker and fade.

MIRROR

If I held a mirror to your image
would I complain if a mist came between?
Would I sing out, Here is a sign!
She is living!
Do you think I would reach for a cloth
to polish the glass where the last drops clung
remembering your breath?

Already it fades.

Now the mirror reflects a landscape
sleeping in winter,
trees ghostly in the dawn,
the earth a supplicant
begging forgiveness.

Who could rise from so long a sleep?
Who would disturb the air that flows
over the pond, the slow fall of leaves
from maple and beech?

Where has your spirit gone?
Would love as strong as ours
not leave a trail behind your vanishing star?

FOR A COMING GRANDCHILD

I know why the black clay cracks
and why it spurns that single drop.
I know why the air splits
and why the shrieking banshees
haunt the trees in May
flaunting torn blossoms in their hair.

I know why
nursery rhymes are better fodder
for a heart made mean by sorrow
than the music of the stars.

I know all this before you are born.
But I will be wise and will hide my knowledge
I will give you blessing but no counsel
I will pray you peace and keep my wisdom
I will leave you space and keep my distance.

May the Gods bless you with her lost grace.

DECADE

Ten years on we are still bereft.
Naked as the trees whose cast-off bones
lie on the grass,
I, a wintry widow, collect
and clear to leave a green space.
We are accustomed to this.
Our faces to each other
over a rake, reflecting loss.
We speak your name often.
Oona.
It could be a bell's chime
rung for a long gone summer.

It speaks of more:
Of daffodils innocent of grief
whose heads bent at the place
where your last breath slipped
into the other world.

SUPERMARKETS

Supermarkets are hardest.
Aisles open their maws
thirsty for grief
near your favourite curry,
lentils, an exotic pomegranate,
its seeds ripened in your flesh.
Its name fed you.
Pomegranate, you sang.

My steps mourn these aisles.
Your hearse
makes its slow way through.

JOURNEY

Strange the ease with which I ponder
the sacred journey you made,
its labyrinthine turns
shafts of sunlight remembered,
dull water brightened by a dazzle
of lilies like young princesses
wearing crowns of gold,
as if nothing could be more natural.
I marvelled at your grace
in the midst of the trivial,
ponds made iridescent
shadowed corners in rooms made luminous
and music everywhere.

I GREET THE STARS EARLY

I greet the stars early
I watch their unanchored drift,
a last echo of angels.

Here sleep the souls of children
whose mothers mourned too long
whose laments split the space
between earth and infinity.
They will travel alone
until time ends and they become
the mote in the spider's eye
the spark in the dying fire.

I know your season.
All the colours we bear
in memory, past autumns
in the tint of hair
skin like moonshine
on winter water
eyes lit with the glow
of summer and feet
lithe as a bird's flight.

Winter came at the end.
All your life's mystery sealed
under its veil.

COMMUNION

God was once here
resting on my red tongue
his pale waxen bread
fed my hunger.

His flesh was grown wheat
in some long meadow
fringing a river, perhaps,
or a wide estuary.

Gently he came in
down my throat's curve.
His strong limbs sang
when I received him.

Unleavened as my youth
and as innocent
his body lay in mine
all of one moment.

White as morning moon,
breast of swan
snow on mountain
new-born lamb.

Christ God I knew
in joy and in pain.
Pray for us two
that we meet again.

... Stretching to the limits
of my awakening spirit ...

RESOLUTION

RESOLUTION

I begin now as I meant to begin
long ago when the world was at spring
and the other seasons were tardily due
and that rough-hewn, unshakeable you
knew nothing of this fine-boned,
hammered-out, bevil-edged, honed,
sadder but wiser me.

All those seasons of harvest lingered,
adjusting their timescales,
waiting for moon-shift,
some sudden, tipping-over
slide-down of pocked surface
into this reaping.

I begin again as I meant to begin
long ago when the centre of things
coiled in itself and itself was me
and the spade idled,
the weeds clambered.
It was enough to be.

LOVE I

Love is an understanding.
Intellect and will
are its steel bones.

When flesh fades,
hues and perfumes too,
steel bones endure.

MOTHER LOVE

This head-flopping, tight-fisted, crumpled thing,
this screwed-up, red-faced bag of wind,
this wide-mouthed, soft-suckling, greedy one,
this ever-wailing, starlight-paling, selfish son,
this nappy-soiling, bib-spoiling,
bed-wetting, wind-fretting
smiled at me today.
Smiled at me today.

First Child

Now all my energies are turned towards you.
My love adorns you with a thousand skills
and all my own suppressed accomplishments
look for fulfilment as your life begins.

What I bequeath you when my own life ends
must not be tarnished by still-born desire
and I must never push a poet's pen
into a hand that burns with other fire.

Though Plato's golden child you yet may be,
how shall I know your gold from painted tin?
How shall I hold you while I set you free
and teach you with both love and discipline?

CREATOR

Everything sparkles now,
marble glistens,
all the brasses glitter
and the silver shimmers
on polished Sheraton.
Floor shines too,
its warm oak catching
the light, refracting
almost to rainbow hues.

Out in the garden harmony prevails.
A last lupin lifts its elegant head,
perfectly enhanced by green,
the sombre laurels are its foil.

Nothing of this was chance.
Landscape and still life
are my compositions. I repose
only to admire,
then flurry to new births,
perhaps even to compose
this poem.

CLONMONEY

Our choice was after all the right one,
to cut ourselves off from the common herd
here, on this platform of green land,
the soil a thin skin on limestone core.

Here, by our love and our sweat, have we
unsheathed the dead spirits from their mould
where they lay hungrily a thousand years,
ringed in by cairn, stone piled on stone.

Their old ash bones lightened our clay,
grew sweet peas against tiered walls.
Their eyes awaited our expected tears,
hearts thudded too at our children's call.

They smell with us the late-seeding grass,
plod by our steps to the milking yard.
Ears leap to listen for first-born calf,
eyes blaze to follow swift-falling star.

Summer heat hazing the leafed-over trees
warms their cold blood in sap and in plant.
So will our veins throb with the wild geese,
blanch with the moon at their grief-laden chant.

BALLAD OF A TOWN

In that cold town where I grew wise,
east winds fretted at our doors,
black hills stood gaunt against black skies,
dark tides assembled off our shores.

Beside the gap where North and South
link in unholy, brief alliance,
my town had bitterness in its mouth
which soured our breath to death's defiance.

Because of memories soaked in gall,
labour and diligence were its pride
when factory smoke lay over all.
It was for this good men had died.

And so the hedge-stitched fields that clung
to Cooley hills and Ravensdale
were splendid anthems to be sung
within a Gaelic, Southern Pale.

Neat gardens and good crops, they said,
are silent victory over drums,
and while they smuggled white North bread
they diligently cleared their slums.

Upon their dreams I turned my back
for softer words and kinder smiles,
for hills that never can look black,
for tides that bleach the rocky miles.

Here winds that blow by west and south
bring rain and storm and singing birds
and bitterness never taints my mouth
and I have learned some kinder words.

Yet sometimes in this gentler land
I feel a rankling in my bones,
dead fathers growl in reprimand
at easy living on Clare stones.

DAUGHTER

Such joy I have not known.
Pleasure in your soft face,
arched brows and skin
flowering to pink.

I gaze, drink to my flesh
the loveliness of yours.
Then mourn my loss
and yours to come.

LOVE II

When clouds clash,
cymbal-sounding in their thunder,
maybe that's love,
Greek Gods lusting after plunder.

When a pale moon spills
yellow light stolen from the sun,
maybe that's love,
Diana hunting for a little fun.

When a poet looks
with no malice on another's dream,
maybe that's love
paddling in the shallows of the stream.

When a poem burns
a hole in the heart or the mind,
maybe that's love
leaving its resting place behind.

When a woman knits
Aran sweaters for her little nieces,
maybe that's love
picking up stitches, smoothing creases.

When a woman sells
her soul and freedom as a wife,
maybe it's love
throws her in the ditches of life.

RESCUE

'I refuse to be used', I said.
'I refuse, refuse to be your muse', I said,
'God'. How he teetered on teetering toes
back to his precipice.
Typically male, he whined,
'your fault if I die'.
'Do what you must', I said,
'it's your own damned dust'.
'Let it be on your head', he said.

A dandelion tickled his toes.
'*Pissenlit*', I said.
'What?' he cried.
'Piss the bed', I explained.

And he fell on his nose.
Laughing, he fell on his nose.

WORDS

Words do not come easily to age.
The garrulous were better silent,
for that rasping repetition
makes mock of the old saying,
wisdom is bought by years.

Words do not come easily to youth.
The wise would keep their peace
when self-expression is but masturbation.
Zealots may rush to revolution
blooded by others' tears.

Words come easily to three-year-olds.
Their vision is still bright.
Let foolish men be still and listen.
Marvel at the tongue
that calls a hanging sock
a waterfall.

SPRING IN MEELICK

Just budding is the willow;
baby finger leaves
open to the warmth of sun.
This noon
is a golden glow.
Daffodils in streams
spill across the lawn,
such green
shimmering with yellow,
innocent as Eve's
first loving look.
No harsh God here.

GERANIUM

That geranium looks poor.
While I was away the dust gathered,
moisture dried in its roots
and the leaves fell, withered.

Even cobwebs, daring, looped
with acrobat's zeal its brittleness,
branches so imprisoned dropped
under the shame of neglect.

So I, motherly, brush
chains of gossamer from its back,
pour water on its shrivelled arms,
make atonement for the others' lack.

They think my geranium is dead.
I should throw it out and plant a new shoot,
but I pick the leaves it shed
and I mulch its root.

Flame red this blossom grew,
once brightening the dark.
A kiss of life might renew
one burgeoning spark.

Breath on its soil I give,
spittle on its limbs,
my image on its coming leaves,
on its flower their sins.

HERETIC

I feel I should apologise,
acutely still aware that penitence
is portion of my past,
cruel precedent for this
inadequate disguise.
I say, 'non credo'.
But not loud,
lest you, who stand beside me,
should be scandalised.
Millstones round my neck
I could not bear,
plunging me to depths of darkest seas,
so I wear
my disbelief in secret flesh,
carry it in conversation where
it touches only, never burns
with frozen fingers
all those tepid lives
who warm themselves at altar fires.

WEDDING PICTURE

You had forgotten the photographer
and that wild man you plucked
from some sleazy side street
obeyed your gay command.
'Take us anyway'.

So there we are, all took
anyway. You laughing,
the guests grinning, I caught
with such a strained, haunted look,
my foot half in the car.

I remember the day.
My French brocade,
the riddles of words,
doors banging in the church,
the white iced cake
a mad Czar's palace,
two prisoners on its roof,
and everyone laughing
except your family,
who wept for loneliness.

And then there was me,
of course, signing the book
with the wide, dazzled look.
I think your photographer was very good.

THAT OLD LOVE AGAIN

Love is a great patience,
it is a long waiting,
an unblossoming tree
reaching out to light.

What young men call love
is a sad substitute.
All aches and pains and groans,
guitar playing to moons.

When a maiden loves
it is a self-deceit,
a vanity adorned
with foolish dreams.

When psalmists sing,
worshipping with words,
they but praise God,
beauty and love,
or sing for the sweet sound
their voices make.

Love is a great patience,
it is a long waiting,
an unblossoming tree
reaching out to light.

IF I FORGET

If I forget the morning light
when sombre night has closed my days
or turn aside because of pride
from the sweet sound of others' praise,
if I shut all my visions out
because a wife and mother must,
will my sad shade be still afraid
to watch the sunshine on my dust?

If I neglect what most I need
in these, my most creative years,
and fill my hours with endless chores,
repetitive to point of tears,
although my labours are for love,
still in my heart the artist lies
when my unselfish days are done.
Will she reproach me then with cries?

INHERITANCE 1970

Our fathers, you say, were stronger, holding vials
of life-procuring liquid in their hands,
gaining, they said, vengeance and immortality at once,
forcing jealous Gods to heed their demands.
This justified the years of eating dirt,
the crumb-picking from swineherds' swill,
the burnt pride hidden under smiles,
the bent knee fostering the urge to kill.

What did they gain, our fathers, stronger than we,
but an extended mortgage on our land,
so that we pay endlessly, endlessly,
and dash the poisoned vial from the hands?
We are unworthy heirs to their unworthy dreams,
forced by unworthy foes to dissipate
our creativity in wasteful schemes,
crying that everything's too little and too late.

IRELAND 1972

Here, we,
dazzled by the returning glare
of our despairing glass,
grasp at straws,
pause
to reflect on
our imperfections,
soothing our guilt,
terror of bombs,
guns at the doorway,
blood on the floor, say
history began it,
others began it.

What's bred in the marrow
comes out in the bone.

Narcissus is thrown
by splintering bone.

KIN

Over in Liverpool and probably Leeds
hundreds of Kelly cousins propagate.
Their nightly hammerings are deeds
not spoken of here. We are less profligate
of our nights. But then we didn't manure
England's streets with our dung, or tear
the living hearts of cities with our fumes
and phantasms, or blaspheme its churches
with our beery prayers. Those cousins knew
the iron wheel, chimneys sky-tall,
cones and tunnels, the fierce heat-smelt,
cement works and underworld of mines,
trains, coal. Lonely for moss and dank rain smells,
hungry for kindred accents, their sweat and
fouled beds built England, and all so that
someday a fat, greasy slut
might slam her dingy door shut
and push a notice before a blinking eye.
'Can't you read, you lot? No Irish need apply'.

And over in the US and even in Trinidad
and in Australia and New Zealand too,
hundreds of Costelloe cousins copulate,
more genteely, I am sure, being tuned
to softer airs, and have given their bright,
glittering eyes and white hair and broad
countenances and their sometimes angry stare
to innocent progeny. Their counsel usually wise,
they have surely passed with mild indifference
along their private paths.

And here, back where it all began,
we come to the end of the track.
You and I, dear, have fallen down on the job,
or left it to others to do the trick.

FEAR

Who will tell my tale when I am done,
my pen faltering finally,
if, long before my mind rots in its bone,
the world I live in closes silently?

FOR A DEAF FRIEND

I have discovered a new voice
which hesitates by my ear.
Its low tone affects me more
than moonlight symphony.

It speaks of a muted life,
the way the drifting leaves
tell of the silenced summer
and the winter-locked fields.

Crocus-bud and chrysalis
sound the same chord
while they work miracles
without a word.

Butterfly and petalled gold
momentarily display
what even saints may not behold,
however long they pray.

Do not disturb your silence
or shatter with spasm of throat
the carefully wrought wonder
of your life's thought.

Lament to Van Gogh

No poet I,
only a dreamer dreaming,
content to idle in the lazy light
of summer evening,
content to watch the changing colour
on sleepy, shadowy field,
to let the murmuring and wonder
tap at my heedless ears.

No painter I,
only a sleeper sleeping,
while all the pearly pillows in the sky
hold loveliness for keeping.
My brush and canvas, pen and paper,
patient, await my touch.
No candles in my hat, no bright taper
will move me to much.

That ritual of denial, self-immolating prayer,
centred their days as Christ could not have done,
could not, even had he bent behind their chair,
praising the tortuous scrolls they had begun.
Thus they adorned his words, fingers twisted in pain,
frothing to blossom head each pious thought,
curving in serpents' tails with cunning care.
The very chastity they had so dearly bought,
not just the skills of their pale, pointed pens
nor the beloved dyes that now illuminate,
and catch our breath to wonder, as even then
it made them smile and look and meditate,
not just their love gave radiance to each page,
so that it leaps to greet us from the text,
humorous and shy, and coyly strange,
by its own divine foolishness perplexed.

'Credo', they sang, limning the angel's face,
lion and eagle and calf posed unperturbed.
'Credo', they sang, and the blue was a jewelled grace,
brilliant with faith, perfect and undisturbed.

Pointless to weep now for their faded lives,
the linnet singing in the raptured elm,
the treacherous seas bearing Viking knives,
sharpened for victory over monkish pen.

ELEGY FOR MARY CATHERINE

Memory strains to bring
her face to focus.
The eyes washed
by eighty winters
to a pale, rain-filtered blue.
Condensed as poetry,
her past seasons
reinforced her image,
private, distilled by reappraisal,
discreet and disciplined.
Her gestures, always so restrained,
flickered to a numb finger-touch.
Her arteries, blocked, dammed the flow
to ears, eyes, tongue.

Deprived of these, she faltered
once only, and groaned,
then touched our hands
in mute apology.

Our forces gathered in a last loving,
with candle and with psalm
obliterating the silence and the dark,
making our arms her catafalque.

TODAY THERE WAS RAIN AGAIN

Today there was rain again
and the garden lay swollen,
squelched underfoot the tormented grasses,
drowned, not complaining,
and the spires in the city all glistened
and the sky was like pitch.

And under the spires and the sky that was pitch
the bishop complained of communion,
explained that disunion was union,
and the press was impressed.

And I, as I neared Thomond Bridge,
passed a tinker child bearing a wreath
to lay on the grave of his father,
who was knifed in the throat by his mother,
and I met Mrs Clery, still weeping,
for the daughter she'd left in safe keeping
had been raped by her father again
and had drowned herself there in the river.

And it rained on the river.
When they brought up her body,
all swollen by water,
like grasses in gardens,
tormented but still uncomplaining.

FEMINIST I

Lucky to have made that leap
out of the dark of youth's complacence,
somewhere encountered the agony
controlled effort wrought within the mind.
Lucky, when others vegetated,
to have refused the lure of acquiescence,
always despising the passive moon
scuttled by sun and rendered half blind.

Lucky to have whorled within
shell-like, encompassing tides,
change and cycle, the avenging sins
of woman's indifference, man's pride.
Lucky to have withstood tears,
passion, pain and all the raw wounds,
the brash, God-despairing, midnight fears,
the hangover of high noons.

Infolded, involuted soul
finally unburdened, turns at ease,
conscious of the years' exquisite toll,
ignoring its fatal disease.

SPINSTER

Not lace-curtained, peering behind
webs of mellowing thread, filtering
light too gaudy for the near blind.
Not that anymore. She needs no pitying.
Her own contempt is not kind
but nonetheless fitting.

Why would you woo her
from early morning drive,
from dedication at a desk,
enchained by nine-to-five,
an extra hour, more or less,
proving her adventurously alive?

Is it so strange that she should shun
your insistence on proffered delights,
love in a semi, your splendid sun
eclipsing her solitary, moonless nights?
And later, more than ever alone,
swollen to ripe-pomegranate size,
anticipating a future she cannot condone
but only tolerate, she develops hopeless eyes.

Watch them in supermarket or bus queue,
eyes embalmed by despair,
impervious to spring or autumn hue,
winter and summer receive the same stare.

Leave her to sterile page and type.
Mechanical words beating a tune,
your kind of love will only wipe
rose-misted spectacles too soon.

MIDDLE AGE

No passion of loss anymore.
Only a faint thread
leads to memory's door,
threatening the unburied dead.

Travel that pale skein
and know it might reveal
pain too great to bear,
love too deep to heal.

Better unravel and let go,
brilliance of day must fade,
though hobbled time is slow
to pull down night's shade.

All storms are mirrored now,
and that's the worst deceit.
Maturity's final blow
is to acknowledge the cheat.

RATIONALE

The stunted blackthorn
thrusts its ruptured limbs
at every passer-by,
and every wind condemns it.
Yet still it stands
with obstinate pretence,
denying it is dead.

All winter I can hear it cry,
all winter long through wet and wild.

I think I'll take the hatchet now,
release its spirit with a final blow,
and later warm my hands upon its flame
and christen its new birth with a new name.

From twisted thorn to fire,
from flaming fire to ash,
from ash to smoke to dust.

Outside upon the tulip bed
the ash will settle well,
and if it cries again
I'll cut off all the tulip heads
and mulch them in the compost heap.
And if it still complains
I'll try again
till I've run out of christening names.

FUNCTIONS

Over and over the heart is impaired
by day's uneasy rhythms.
A boy's scowl across a meal
jolts again, although familiar.
Night's repose is seldom spared
reminders of fatal decay.
Each fibrillating, nervous beat
stammers across bridges of dismay.

Blood is still rash to circulate,
indolent, unaware,
feeding flesh insatiate
while mind breeds despair.

NOON-DAY TIGER

I bargain for life now, feel the huckster's dread
of the short change, the quick sleight of hand
that might unload some goods I need
to keep me profitable. Few quick gambles
tighten my muscles or add fire to eyes
too used to counting costs.
Weighing and measuring, balancing this for that,
avoiding common colds, draughts and muscles overstrained,
dreading sudden bankruptcy.

Do not misunderstand me. I am not afraid
of airless nights. Lungs solidified, I can lie
perfectly still and take shallower breaths,
hoard the penurious bubbles of my life
for days when deeper breaths may justify,
by their existence, this too-thrifty care.

No church can heal me as one did
when, young and supplicant, I sought sanctuary
and in warm shadows and dim lights I hid
with polished timbers and sad imagery
of saints who never once unveiled their dreaming eyes
or paled with pain to hear my foolish cries.

If some strange God could bend again
to stroke away the quivering and the fears,
terror of dark, death and all the unknown,
the bleak future and the beckoning years,
what would it find with that first, tentative touch
on flesh that worshipped spirit overmuch,
but middle-aged complacence, unafraid,
voice of a psalmist with the hymns unsung,
echo of martyr, unquartered and unhung.

Mind of a mystic, contemptuous of myths,
heart of a poet, bored by poets' tricks.
Pardon me, spirit, if I remove
my chains of unrequited love
and don the flesh of middle age
with all the resignation of a sage.
Mock, if you like, my careful husbandry,
each second ploughed and tilled, and produce weighed,
showing achievement of such little worth.
I too deride the little life I've made.

Feminist II

All the words to do with underthings
applied to us. Devious, subtle, snaring,
underwear. All that hidden growth,
stifled, suffocating, but of course caring.
Oh how we cared! Our tears, rotted through mulched depths,
were activators in that stagnant swamp,
that fermenting compost of our grievance.
Fossil fuels of rage pressed tight,
awaiting the liberating thrust
of common knowledge. Then there was light,
better than strength. That was our gain.
But first there was the pain.

With all of us there was the same quest,
hedged in by nods and knowing looks.
Who could blame our retreat
into boglands of deceit
where, buried even deeper in complaint,
we drowned in layers of prejudice,
praying to be pure and patient?
Even the plea brought new taint.

Our odours were more substance than ourselves,
our images more real than our flesh.

New House

Defying newness, I throw down
a carpet, worn, well marked,
and the table in my room
is used, much loved and therefore scarred.
I am careless too of dotted finger pies
on paint gloss and brash skins
of polystyrene, plastic and the like.
A cobweb is a friend crept in,
lured less by old, familiar dust
than by the sandstorms left
where woodblock floors are grained
and smoothed to camouflage,
denying old, more noble ancestry.

Last week the mice invaded,
tunnelled through cement,
skipped past open doorways,
wore hobnailed boots as always
when they ranged above the ceiling.
I was moved to fury
at their crass possession,
shrieked when hand touched one,
soft in a drawer of scarves.

Why did I weep, recalling
that old and mildewed house
now making private protest
at mice and southwest gales?

HALF CENTURY

Others have not been lucky as we
who have shared these generous times,
welding together even in absence
every present moment, so that we become
almost one flesh, each self-sufficient
though interdependent. Siamese twins.
It would not be true to say there have been
no rows, no flurry of disparate views,
flaring to rooftop high
our loud sundering of old vows.
They have been rare and only memorable
because of that.
Yet our lives have not been placid –
the usual deaths, the common griefs,
the surge and swell of children,
bad school reports, drugs in a window box,
even the policeman at the door.

When I look back through my half century
I am astonished to discover
that for only half of it
I have known you. The other half
collapses on itself by this default.
That first growth seems in retrospect
a kind of vagrancy, a maverick uncertainty
without anchorage. An unrewarded search.

I am overwhelmed by the dicey chance of this.

Other lovers write in praise
or in cherished recall of the intimacies
which, being secret, are shattered by a phrase.
I cannot describe the puzzle we have made,
jig-sawing miraculously, fitting our variety,

our patchwork lives, our woven cloth,
many-textured, many-coloured, into this tent
with which we clothe and house ourselves.

These are the things we have together made,
gardens and houses, walls I know will stand
long after we are gone. Vistas have opened
and closed to our command,
and the buttressed land has been breached
and yielded a little. All may remain
when we unfold ourselves in twin plots
and return separately to that dust
which gave us common sustenance. It is a grief
I dare not ponder, our separate deaths.
Will we, I wonder, for the next half
of half a century, with unexplored insight
unwind, unfold, untangle twined-over roots from roots,
unravel time itself so that we may slide
placidly back to birth, and finally divide?

All those unsayable words
you, being private, regard as sacred
will have found their place.
Can these things we have made
speak of them, our loves, our fears, our griefs?
Or the nonsensical breakfast discussions,
politics, the day's bombings, the brute maimings,
the tattered fabric of our outer lives?
Is that what we will leave?

Lovers who are permitted
mirrored glimpses of each other
forget the privilege and become familiar.

We have somehow escaped such despair,
are constantly amused by the absurd.
Perhaps we share
a half-witted simpleness
and regard the world
through the other's innocence.

STARLINGS

The starlings are aggrieved
and rancorously complain,
returning to high-treed,
beech-bowery domain,
when I in innocence,
with basket and with bowl,
by blackcurrant paths advance
to breach their harvest hoard.

Have I not got the right,
since mine the back that bent,
the energy to fight,
the mind with true intent,
that conjured up this bower,
these paths, that pond, that fence,
and every nodding flower?

Must I be dispossessed
by mere belligerent birds
while every sluggish pest
turns strawberries to curds,
while greenfly sucks the blood
of the tender baby rose
and dahlias die in bud
as the greedy earwig grows?

There is a time to make a stand
or lose a kingdom hardily won.
A gardener and an emperor
may never idle in the sun.

HORIZONS

A green slope strides the horizon,
banishing distance.
A mountain is curved
and crowned with fuzz
of new-leafed trees
canopied by a mushroom sky.

Horizon inhibits but never stems
the stride of hills.
Veering to blue
in silvery, distant haze,
a river lurks, a railway track
severs another landscape,
and the pocking chimney-stacks
signify housewifery tending fires,
smoke pluming from their altars.

My mind, translucent, enters hills,
unscrambles clouds, is boundless.

WINTER DAY

A long time ago there were passions,
unruly rumblings would erupt
time and time again. Tears and rage.
Lovely the furies that dismembered thought
and the cool harmonies of self.
Then – a long time ago it seems – there's
a sudden shift of snow
bringing a thrush in speckled surprise
from slaty, sleeting skies. That would stir,
move the heart, pulse leap, pupil dilate
and God knows what else as the body stood
transfixed by love, tormented and ecstatic.
A long time ago, before lover or child,
kitchen leavings, the debris of peelings,
crumbs, a sodden teabag, there were springs
of season as of soul. Why now do tears rise
again? Glad drops recall those mad,
rushing-out days, wellington boots to the
river in flood and a cargo ship chug-chugging
up from Kilrush and nothing in the head
but the joy of life – a great skinful.
What now? Bespectacled over book print,
arthritic even with the garden trowel,
obsessed with cleanliness and food for mouths,
housewife, housewife, housewife, that's all.

And December closing in freezes the cabbage stalks,
brings a russet bird to challenge snow,
flame against white, passion against thought,
flamboyant celebration. Here I am,
here I am, here I am.

LOVE LETTER

You're away a full week now.
The house is still, still.
I'm getting used to the silence,
the throttled radio on the window sill.

Outside the bees are barmy,
zipping along the apple flowers,
and the day is definitely balmy,
and I leave doors open all hours.

I sit here in this little corner,
the rest of the house stretching its rooms,
empty as a city after fire,
and the garden blooms, blooms.

The birds have gone bananas in the trees –
the dawn chorus was a full brass band.
There's no one snoring in my bed.
Everything is grand, grand.

I found that clean shirt you missed.
Will I post it up today?
If it's with this letter, I did,
if not, it's on its way.

The children are fine,
doing their own thing,
you-know-who moody as hell.
Today is the last day of spring.

Don't kill yourself with work.
There's no need to phone.
The dandelions look great on the lawn.
When are you coming home?

TREES

I could worship God if I were a tree,
raising my arms in prayer
just like the sycamore there.
I planted it with you.
I planted all the others too,
chestnuts from seed,
oak, birch, beech,
mountain ash and the pines,
a sentinel each.
But I never thought to see
the elevated branches of our tree
glorifying God for me.

The chestnut knows its proper role.
Notice the modesty of its stance,
mild as a maid attending her first dance,
faintly scented, flowers yet to unfold,
drooping a hundred handkerchiefs by chance,
signals to lovers ready for romance.

I prefer trees who communicate with God,
whose leaves are hymns of eloquence,
whose golden blossoms sing 'Amen, amen',
whose dreams reflect His mysteries.

Three generations before me knew this shore,
gouged the soft sand under toes,
full cockles swivelling to avoid
inevitable capture. I think of them
only in passing and, still thoughtless,
pluck the cockles from their beds.

Earlier I pondered over tombs,
ancestral names well chiselled in stone,
the gravedigger chuckling to himself
as he hooked back bramble ends,
wild weeds and herbs, child-high.

Everywhere the Twelve Bens towered.
Our grave was picked to catch the view –
mountains to head, ocean to feet,
and the dead lie replete.

Last night I lay awake. The midnight sun
languished over Inishbofin.
All year I wished for this,
high summer, late June,
and the days' exquisite lingering.
Through winter dark my thought
Touched this undying light.

Today I hear you died last night.

There was nothing sudden in your end.
Predicted and expected, each day's diagnosis
a sad confirmation. Still you lingered,
said you couldn't bear to miss a thing,
Christmas parties, Patrick's Day parades,
brass bands trumpeting through spring.

It was like you to claim this day,
to eke out the sun,
trail with it shadowless over the edge,
slip from bright consciousness to oblivion,
just when the last glimmer struck the fuchsia hedge.
Then, right on time,
no second wasted,
up came the dawn.
That was your cue.
And you missed it.

Your bubbling life rattled to its close
in a bitter pun. Too desperate for air,
your blood struggled to be free,
and stained as it rose
the pale dawn of your skin,
the night of your hair.

November is the proper month for this,
decline and decay, the colours of death
explicit on the trees, the soft kiss
of rain treacherous in every breath.

But you chose high summer. It hardly seems fair
that the trees should hang out banners and rejoice
in green triumphalism. No hint of despair
in all this luscious sap-swilling. The tipsy voice
of the skylark celebrates its own birthday
and, hovering high, the hawk
hangs, death for its victim a drop away.
While only the butterfly trembles on its stalk.

There is not much left of illusion any more.
Seasons betray, lovers are fickle, children grow strange.

Good friends are hard to come by, treasures to store
with memories to cherish. Oh, death brings no change,
is nothing new, only an old joke repeated,
a vanishing trick, a sudden spur to the heart,
a whimsical telling that we are born defeated,
finished before we get a chance to start.

I remind myself of all of this and explore
the ravages mortality enjoins,
the gaps unfilled, the parents gone before,
the gold-minted children dulled to false coins.
So the empty cradle and the dispossessed chair
are relics to be auctioned, with a love-inscribed book,
a silver christening mug, some Minton ware,
a wedding photograph for a dealer's look.

These are the greatest source of pain, these imprints
of the dead. The effervescent voice is only an ache
echoing through the ear, the quick glance a lost hint
of old vibrance. Possessions too solidly make
tangible hurt. Discarded on a beach,
ravaged cockle shells are a child's rejected treasure.
Soon, soon, soon you will be out of reach,
our loss impossible to measure.

COGNOMENS

I have a friend who calls her uterus her gearbox,
and this unlikely terminology
clanking aeons away from the Greek,
somehow gives her comfort. She can then laugh
at the shifts and changes which transport her,
protesting, but inexorably, on her journey
away from wooden horses and towards –
one must assume – rockets and new moons.

I am less happy with mechanical notions,
can adjust only with abstract eye
to marvels of engineering, admire for their nerve
iron obscenities that profane the landscape,
litter even the chaste canopy
which mutes our sunlight and rainbow-bridges trees.

My obsession is named Tiger.
Grr, grr, she growls intermittently in her cage,
sometimes stretches and yawns,
velvety smooth, pulsating with power,
langorous and warm.
Prr, prr, prr. Stroke me and I will neck-nuzzle,
gnaw you into passion, devour with kisses
and lick and lollop, slavering for love.

I sleep with my Tiger, because
her eyes have watched the moon give birth,
she has swallowed sunlight
and made the rainbow dark.

Another wet day, the sky closed in,
rumours of death everywhere,
a shoot-out in Cavan with the IRA,
Greenham Common women weep in despair.

Somewhere there's a button to be pressed,
code words recited, and a flicking thumb
will set the air on fire. We know the rest.
Death may be slow or quick, but it will come.

I don't know why we've done it, God.
I don't understand the pain.
Perhaps if I listened for a thousand years
someone might explain.

But I haven't got the time, God,
and that's the plain truth.
I threw some of it away on you, God,
and some of it on youth.

Feminist III

This silence has been
a sore thing, grievous even.
At times it seemed
nothing would restrain
its fury and flame.
Banked down, smouldering,
might it now shower
someday on the innocent
rockets of power,
Catherine-wheel fragments?

Conspiracy makes conscript,
battens within,
no share in storm,
motions of life,
reasonable rage,
each prick an insult taken in,
quietly absorbed.
Hard to remain sane
and hold what silence must contain.

If revolution should come,
think what utterance would undo.
Kindly condescension out the door,
martyrs and mothers redundant,
male poets losing monopoly,
punch-ups for women on the cards.
I can think of two
whose noses it would pleasure to blood.

And even, even (can it be dreamed?),
no lone scream in the night's heart,
no joke or poet's debate,

Leda and swan, Benny Hill, bar-stool show,
insidious marks of cloaked hate.

Well, lips are padlocked still.
Speech too grave for song
breaks another rule of tongue.
Open lips are for kissing.

Paint them for that.

ABOUT THE AUTHOR

Maeve Kelly was born in Ennis, Co. Clare and educated in
Dundalk. She trained as a nurse in St Andrew's Hospital,
London and, after qualifying, worked in Oxford, before
returning to Ireland. For many years she lived and farmed
with her husband, Gerard O'Brien Kelly and children,
Joseph and Oona, in County Clare. She became involved in
the women's movement in 1974 and was a founding
member of the Limerick Refuge for Battered Wives, now
called Adapt House, where she was administrator for
fifteen years. She was also a founder of the Limerick
Federation of Women's Organisations and the National
Federation of Refuges. She initiated a major work of
research on violence against women entitled *Breaking the
Silence*. She has worked with RTÉ.

Maeve is the author of two novels: *Necessary Treasons*
(Michael Joseph, 1985) and *Florrie's Girls* (Michael Joseph,
1989) and two short story collections, *A Life of Her Own*
(Poolbeg Press, 1976) and *Orange Horses* (Michael Joseph,
1990), also a satirical feminist fairytale, *Alice in Thunderland*
(Attic Press, 1993) and two collections of poetry, *Resolution*
(Blackstaff Press, 1986) and *Lament for Oona* (Astrolabe
Press, 2005). Her short stories have been widely
anthologised, have been translated into many European
languages and broadcast on BBC and RTÉ. In 1972 she
won a Hennessy Literary Award.